Are You Kidding?

John Sant'Ambrogio

Publishing assistance by BookCrafters,
Parker, Colorado.
www.bookcrafters.net

Dedicated to my children

Stephanie
Sara
Michael

and my grandchildren

Bella
Brie
Sebastian

Ski Town USA, Painting by Gregory Block.

Chapter I

Chad had just bought the house of his dreams in Old Town, Steamboat Springs, Colorado. Old Town is that section of Steamboat Springs where the early settlers first built. The house was nice, but the location, location, location was the answer to his dreams. Chad loved to ski, to hike, to mountain bike, and he enjoyed the friendly atmosphere that a small town emanated.

Chad, who was always smiling and friendly to everyone, was of solid build with blond hair and had an engaging manner about him. Chad was the kind of person that loved to be around other friendly people, and he was always reaching out to others.

After four days of moving all his stuff into his new place and unpacking, he decided he would take a short break before getting back to the intense and unusual work that he needed to do. So, during a pause in his work schedule, he began to knock on his neighbors' doors and introduce himself. When he rang the bell of the house right next to his, he was surprised to hear someone yell from an upstairs window.

"Hi neighbor, the door is unlocked. Come on in—I'm upstairs on a ladder replacing a light bulb. I just saw you walk over from next door."

Chad was delighted, opened the door and started to walk upstairs. He thought to himself, *Wow, this must be a safe neighborhood. This guy doesn't even lock his door.*

When Chad reached upstairs, he saw a tall, slim, dark haired, handsome man carefully getting down off the ladder. As he reached the floor, the man thrust out his hand and said, "Hi, I'm Bryan. Glad to meet you, neighbor."

"I'm Chad. Hey, glad to meet you, too. I just moved in next door, and I thought I'd try to meet my new neighbors."

"Wow, that's what I did last week. I just moved in, too."

Chad was aghast. "Are you kidding?"

"No, I'm not kidding. I've been trying to move here for several years. I love to ski, bike and hike, and there isn't any better place than here to do all that."

"Holy cow, those are the same things I love to do," Bryan humorously responded. "Now you are the one really kidding."

Chad jumped in, "Come on, who would move here if they didn't like to ski?"

Bryan offered, "Just look around. There's a heck of a lot else going on here besides skiing. This place has hiking, biking, theatre, music, even opera. In fact, I read that Steamboat ranked third in the country for arts vibrancy in a small town. And it has terrific restaurants like Harwigs, where they sometimes have a local string quartet perform for their guests, but the nicest thing about the small town is the pilgrim attitude. Its people like to explore. Neighbor, this is really great. With our mutual interests, we could be buddies and explore the mountains together."

Chad smiled and said, "Sounds wonderful. We just have to get it all in with my huge work schedule."

Bryan was quiet, "I'm not kidding, but I have the same problem. Chad, what do you do?"

"I'm a scientist."

Bryan looked so surprised, "I am too! I teach astrophysics at the college."

"Bryan, now you really must be kidding," Chad said.

"What kind of scientist are you?" Brian asked.

"I work as a chemist," Chad replied.

Chad and Bryan shook hands again, and then Chad ran down the stairs knowing he had a heck of a lot to do if he was going to complete the incredible tasks before him. One, that unknown to him, was going to place him in great danger.

Fish Creek Falls.

Chapter II

After a week of toil, Chad was able to get his studio set up for the needs his complex project required. After finally putting all instruments he needed in his new lab, he took a moment to rest on his living room couch. After five minutes of leisure, there was a knock on his door, and he could see through the window that it was Bryan.

"Hi, Bryan, what are you up to?"

"Oh, I was wondering if you'd like to take a short walk up the trail by Fish Creek Falls? Some locals told me it was a fun hike."

"You know what? —that sounds great. I bet with your tall height and long legs, you are going to outpace me. I need to get out because I've been inside too long. I need nature. Perhaps when we return, we could have supper at one of the great restaurants in town you've been telling me about."

"Fantastic!" Bryan shouted.

After their three-hour hike up and down the Fish Creek Falls trail, they went downtown for supper at Mambo Italiano, a great Italian restaurant.

"Amazing," Chad commented, "this small mountain town has so much to offer its pioneers. I'm wondering how you found out about it, Bryan?"

"Oh, like a lot of us, I came to ski and fell in love with it. As you saw today on our hike, the scenery is gorgeous with all its mountain streams and rivers. You can drive an hour or two outside of town and the landscape changes in many different ways. But it's always beautiful. Acres and acres of hay fields dotted with beautiful horses, steer and deer between the mountains. Of course, you can see the Continental Divide when you hike some of our mountains. Just stay away from the bears, ha. If one crosses over your path, just raise your arms and growl, and they will run away. I did that one day two years ago while I was visiting and that technique worked, by the grace of God."

Chad laughed, "Oh my goodness. Were you scared?"

Bryan also laughed, "No, it all happened so fast. I got a picture of him with my phone as he ran away. Only later, when I realized what just happened, did I get scared!"

"Well, Buddy, it looks like we both love nature. I'm so glad I moved next to you. What else do you like?"

Bryan quickly responded, "Everything!"

"You're kidding?" Chad responded.

"No, I'm not kidding, Chad. I love all kinds of music, tennis, theatre, art, and my students. Oh, but I don't like politics, and I should add, I like women, and I'm forty years old."

"Bryan, now I know you are kidding. I'm forty years old, too. Did you go on Facebook and find out what I like?" Chad chuckled. And he went on, "I love all those things too and also women. Though I love women, I haven't dated much because I'm always too busy. Most women won't put

6

up with my schedule. As Gary Chapman says in his book, *The Five Love Languages*, your partner wants quality time. I haven't had time to spare. Maybe in the future I will."

Bryan jumped in, "I know you're not kidding because I had the same problem. I wonder if we could buy quality time at Walmart?"

While they both laughed and shook hands, they were filled with gratitude as they left the restaurant.

Chad drove them home. Bryan yelled over to Chad from his front porch before opening his door, "Alright, when our workloads let up, let's get together and enjoy all the things that this incredible town has to offer."

How did this ever happen? Two guys of the same age, both scientists, who have the same interests, come from different parts of the country and they move in next to each other. Boy, the future looked like it was going to be so much fun for them both. Oh, by the way, they had everything in common except for one very important thing.

Chapter III

After two weeks of hard work, Chad rang Bryan's doorbell. No answer. He walked around the house and was surprised to see Bryan trimming the tomato plants in his garden.

"Hey Bryan, how'd ya like to hike up to the Flat Tops tomorrow? Neighbors have told me they are gorgeous and at the top of one mountain, there is something called Devil's Causeway. If you are brave enough, maybe you can join me and walk across it. They say it's only about four feet wide with close to a 1,000 foot drop off on either side."

"Chad, you must be kidding. I've heard all about this, too, but you really want to walk across it? I hear it's jagged and uneven and you have to almost crawl across it. Oh, I don't want you to be braver than me. Let's do it. Come over in the morning, and I'll drive us there."

Bryan and Chad each went to bed early preparing for the exciting event they were planning to do the next day.

After a good big breakfast in town, they hopped in Bryan's car and started their journey. It was a beautiful sunny day in late September, and the trees were so glorious. Gold, yellow and orange leaves mixed with shades of green spruce and pine painted the mountainsides.

"Wow, this is fantastic. I'm sorry you can't enjoy it like me, Bryan. You have to keep your eyes on the road."

"Don't worry, I can see it all fine, and I've got great peripheral vision. I had to develop it for my classes so I could tell if my students on the opposite side of the room were cheating on their tests," he said smiling wryly, "and look, a lot of the view is right in front of us."

After about an hour of driving through the spectacular countryside, they arrived at the Stillwater Reservoir parking lot at the beginning of the Flat Tops Trail. The buddies packed their backpacks with water and a snack and started walking up the mountain. They were in for some surprises.

Oh, Mr. Bear, that's my food.

Chapter IV

The first surprise was a mother bear with two black cubs crossing the trail about ten yards in front of them. They froze. The mother black bear stared at them for thirty seconds and then the two adorable cubs started walking toward them. Chad and Bryan stayed frozen. Then the mother ran after her babies and nudged them up the path and into the woods. Chad and Bryan breathed a sigh of relief.

"Bryan, shall we keep going?"

"Yes, I think we're all right. This is not the Tetons where Grizzlies attack people all the time. Unless we chase her cubs, I don't think she'll trouble us. The only animals that attack humans here are the moose and mountain lions."

Ten minutes later, as they passed a field just left of the trail, there were three moose enjoying the green grass. Again, the buddies froze. The moose didn't even notice them, but Chad and Bryan stooped over and almost crawled on the path until they were out of sight of the big black animals.

After another hour of exhilarating hiking, they reached the top of the mountain and the beginning of Devil's

Causeway. They sat on a rock for a moment to rest as they had worked up a sweat. Bryan took off his hat to let the wind rustle his brown hair and dry the perspiration off his handsome face.

Bryan offered to lead the way, and off they went. They crawled along the causeway, gripping each rock as they worked their way across the terrifying drop-off. They stopped every few minutes to enjoy the incredible and spectacular scenes they could view for miles around them. They finally made it to the other side of the divide. Just as Chad neared the end of the causeway, he stood up and foolishly began to jump off one of the last rocks--and then he slipped. He found himself hanging on the edge of one of the rocks.

"Oh no!" Chad screamed.

"Hang on," Bryan yelled and with incredible speed and dexterity, Bryan got to the other side of Chad and reached down and grabbed Chad's belt and pulled him up to safety.

They sat down on the flat edge where they were both safe and sat quietly for a few minutes.

Chad put his hand on Bryan's shoulder and said, "How can I thank you, Bryan? You may have saved my life."

"I didn't, the good Lord did. I didn't think what to do. I was just impelled by a force greater than me to do whatever it was I did."

They were both quiet for a few minutes more, and then Bryan said, "Should we go back? Are you up to it?"

"Ha, if you stay right behind me, I'll do it, and I promise to be much more careful. Besides, I heard there is a great diner in Yampa where we can stop at on our way back to Steamboat. We can get a root beer float and a hamburger there. That will make me really cautious to stay alive as we cross the causeway so I can enjoy my favorite drink."

They made it back across the causeway and down the mountain safe and sound. They stopped in Yampa at Penny's Diner for the treat they were yearning for—a root beer float. Wow, that was just one more thing these two buddies shared a mutual love for. As they enjoyed their supper together, they started a fascinating discussion that would be carried on for several months.

Is he going to make it across Devil's Causeway?

Chapter V

While enjoying their supper at Penny's, Chad said, "Hey, Bryan, there is something you often seem to bring into your conversation—something that interests me."

"What's that, Chad?"

"You name God as a source of your actions. So, you must believe in God. I want to, but I don't seem to think there is one. I guess you'd call me an agnostic."

"Chad, whatever you are, you are a great guy and a very moral guy. Yeah, I do believe in God. And I am convinced that God loves you even if you don't think He's around. Hey, you want some ketchup on your hamburger?"

"Bryan, what is your religion?"

"Well right now I'm searching the Scriptures and also searching many different religions. I'm struck that there are so many commonalities between many of them. Love seems to be the core of most despite the fact they also have many differences. But the more I search, the more I feel God's presence."

"Bryan, we really seem to get along, and I feel a great

trust in you. There's something I'm tempted to tell you that I can't let out to the world yet. Would you mind if I told you what that is? And if so, I would pray you—okay, I used that word—interesting. I would hope you will never let the secret out."

"Sure, Chad, everything stays here—or maybe safe in my basement."

They both laughed, and then Chad looked down at the table and was quiet.

"Bryan, I'm presently doing a lot of research on the product of a huge pharmaceutical company whose name I won't disclose at this time. There is a suspicion, and a strong belief, that in many of the drugs they are producing there are ingredients, not listed, which are extremely addictive. I have been putting together scientific evidence, after analyzing their drugs, that is proving what has been suspected all along. There are unmentioned addictives in their products. The company is doing incredibly well, and if the truth comes out about what they are doing, it will be a disaster for the company.

"Currently, I'm working with a law firm as we prepare a case against the drug company. One of the reasons I am telling you now is the head of the law firm I'm working with on the project has warned me that it is always possible one of the executives in the pharmaceutical company might secretly hire someone to try to stop my efforts, and maybe I am in danger of something tragic happening to me. So—I want to warn you about what could happen in the future. I don't want you to be in danger also. You might want to reconsider whether or not you want to continue our friendship until the case comes to trial and is decided."

"Oh Chad, Buddy, don't even think about it. You are doing a great thing. I can see your goal is to help mankind, and I'm with you all the way. I'm so honored you would share all of this with me."

They finished their meals and picked up their root beer floats they had been anticipating and clinked their glasses with a toast to a better world—a world without murders.

Unfortunately, there was at least one potential murderer lurking in the shadows.

Gold and green as Fall begins.

Chapter VI

In spite of Bryan and Chad's demanding workloads, they kept getting together for fun activities. They were both bikers and until the ski season arrived, they wanted to bike all over Routt County together. Exhausted after their frequent thirty-mile journeys through the mountains, they'd have supper together.

Another thing they had in common was they both loved to cook, probably because they had been single for so long. But that was going to change soon, and what was about to happen was unbelievable. They really enjoyed preparing great meals for each other at this point in their lives. Their friendship meant so much to each of them.

Chad's work was still quite intense, and it looked like things were not going to come together for another month.

Bryan was also working hard, and what turned out to be so much fun for the buddies was when Bryan invited three or four students from his classes to come and have supper with him and Chad.

Then one day in the cafeteria Bryan met a lovely woman, Laura, who was a faculty member in the history department.

She was attractive with beautiful auburn hair, slim, and quite tall like Bryan. They talked every so often at lunch and Bryan soon found out she was single. He was tempted to ask her out, but he was very shy when it came to asking women for a date.

At supper one night, Bryan told Chad of his dilemma, and Chad encouraged him to invite her to supper with them.

So, the next day Bryan walked over to the table where Laura was sitting alone, and said, "How'd you like to have dinner with my best friend and me?"

Laura replied, "Sounds like fun, but would you also be open to inviting my twin sister, Sandy, who lives with me? We love doing things together."

Bryan was shocked. "You have a twin sister? Hey, is she as pretty as you?"

"No, prettier than me," Laura laughed.

"Bring her along."

"Okay, now this really sounds like fun."

Bryan rushed home after his last class and ran over to Chad's house. He opened the door and yelled to Chad, who he knew was working upstairs, "Hey Buddy, you won't believe what just happened."

Chad came downstairs and he had a real curious look on his face. "What Happened?"

"I invited Laura for supper tomorrow, and she's bringing her twin sister."

"Oh, stop it—you must be kidding."

"No, I'm not!"

So, they ran over to Bryan's kitchen and began exploring all the possibilities they could come up with for a great meal. They were confident they could put a wonderful meal together, but they were also going to be in for a surprise the next day.

Chapter VII

It was getting close to six o'clock the next day—everyone's scheduled time for the exciting dinner. Chad and Bryan felt sure they had put together a great feast for their guests. Then the doorbell rang, and the guys rushed to the door. Standing there were two lovely ladies, but they did not look like twins.

Bryan greeted them and said to Laura, "Well, I'm sorry your sister couldn't come, but I'm glad you brought a friend. She's welcome."

Laura laughed, "This is my twin sister, Sandy, but we're fraternal twins, not identical."

Then Sandy joked, "As you can see, Laura is 'Ms. Tallie,' and I'm 'Ms. Shorty.' And while Laura has reddish hair, mine is blond."

"Oh, I get it. Chad and I aren't identical either."

"You are twin brothers? Oh, I get it—you are kidding. One of you is the best looker—but I won't tell you which one is until we have dessert."

Sandy jumped in with, "I can see we are having a kidding contest here."

They all chuckled and went into the living room and sat down on the two couches.

Chad asked, "Would anyone like a drink?" Everyone responded with "Water for me."

Then he asked Sandy, "What do you do?"

"I'm a lawyer."

"Oh, that sounds fascinating," Chad replied. "I'll bet you have a demanding schedule, like me. I'm a chemist and spend a lot of time working in my lab."

Sandy commented, "I know what that's like. I spend a lot of time writing articles for publication when not helping my clients."

Then Bryan got up and said, "Let's continue this interesting discussion at dinner."

They went into the dining room, and the ladies sat down. Bryan and Chad went to the kitchen and brought the food to the table.

Laura said, "The steak looks great, but I'm a vegetarian."

Bryan and Chad opened their mouths and were shocked.

"Hey, I win the kidding contest—I'm not a vegetarian—or at least not tonight," Laura exclaimed.

They all laughed and started enjoying the great dinner. The buddies and the twins couldn't stop talking, eating and laughing. They were having a great time. Then it was time for dessert and as Bryan brought in four pieces of cherry pie with ice cream, Laura stood up and said, "The best-looking man in this room is…" there was a pause, "whoever that man is whose picture is on the wall over there."

"Oh, stop it, Laura. Abraham Lincoln isn't a better-looking man than me," Bryan argued.

"Maybe not, but I bet he was a better lawyer than you are a scientist."

Everyone couldn't stop laughing. After finishing the dessert, they cleared the table and went into the kitchen. Bryan tried to do the dishes, but Sandy took over. Laura pushed the buddies out of the room and told them to sit on the sofa and relax. "You cooked us a great meal—let us tidy up."

It was a great evening for everyone, and after walking the ladies out to their car, Bryan and Chad waved to Laura and Sandy as they drove off. The buddies looked at each other and smiled.

"Wow, that was fun," Chad said.

"Yeah, it was. It made me think perhaps I should give women some quality time at this point in my life," Bryan responded.

"I guess that's what I got out of the evening, too. Maybe we should go to Walmart and buy some quality time really cheap," Chad joked.

As they drove home, the twins had a similar discussion.

The cattle love to roam in the fields...not the mountains.

Chapter VIII

Soon, once a week the buddies and the twins got together for great meals, kidding contests and Scrabble. This didn't stop Bryan and Chad from getting together two or three times a week to eat and talk. Little by little their discussions got longer and longer. They spent little time on politics even though they both were on the same side of the aisle. They loved nature, history, art, music, and theatre and were so grateful they had moved in next to each other. It was rewarding for them after a strenuous workday to have the chance to talk with a friend about what they loved.

Gradually, some talk began to be about God and did He really exist? Chad so wanted to believe, and Bryan so wanted to convince his new best friend to understand what was real—well at least to him.

They were friendly discussions and Bryan did not push too hard, but he could see Chad really wanted to be convinced of God's existence, but nothing seemed to assure him there was a God.

One night as they finished dinner at Bryan's, Bryan asked, "Doesn't it impress you that we have the sun just at the right distance so we here on earth don't burn up or freeze? If the sun was either a little closer or a little farther away, we'd all burn up or freeze to death. And how about the perfect gravity we have? The earth is just the right size and rotating at just the right speed to give us the perfect gravity we are blessed with. We don't fly off the ground as we would on the moon. If the earth was larger, we might not be able to get up out of our seats to wash the dishes that we couldn't even lift up. Our cars would be stuck on the road."

Chad laughed and replied, "Oh come on! You must be kidding. There is a very important word in our language called 'Coincidence.' Coincidences happen all the time. These coincidences are a result of scientific laws. It's just a coincidence that the moon is in this perfect place in our universe, that the stars are not too close. It's just a coincidence that you and I moved in next to each other—don't you believe that?"

Bryan replied with good humor, "No, God sent me here to bug you."

They both laughed and got up and cleared the dishes.

As Chad started to go home and was walking out the front door, he stopped and realized there was a car in front of his house with a lone driver in it. He stood still and stared at the car, and the driver stared at him for a moment. Then the driver started the car and shielded his face as he quickly drove away.

Chad was shocked. He walked back into Bryan's living room and sat on the couch. Bryan came in from the kitchen and noticed the sullen look on Chad's face.

"What wrong, Chad? You don't look like your usual cheerful self."

"I just saw something that has shocked me and has me worried."

"What?"

"There was a car by my house and the driver was staring at me. He drove off immediately when he realized I had seen him. Maybe that drug company knows what I'm doing and is sending this guy to try to scare me."

"Wow, you may be right, Chad. Did you get his license plate number? What kind of car was it?"

"Are you kidding? I was in too much shock to notice the make of the car. I was focusing on the possibility that someone was trying to scare me."

"You know, I think that's exactly what he probably was trying to do—scare you. No company would get involved in a killing, but they wouldn't hesitate to use fear to get you to stop your work. Do you want to call the police?"

"No, not yet. But, Bryan, don't you want to take a break in our friendship?"

"Are you kidding? No, not yet. When this character wants to join us for supper, maybe."

Bryan's humor lifted Chad's spirits and he went home filled with gratitude that coincidence had given him such a great friend.

Chapter IX

The autumn scenery was astounding. So, the twins and the buddies decided to take a Saturday drive through the beautiful countryside and enjoy the vivid red, orange and yellow colors that covered the mountains.

They went past Clark and then took Seedhouse Road to hike the Gilpin Lake Loop in the Zirkel wilderness. The hike went well, and they made it back to the car after walking five and a half hours.

"All right everybody, how about supper at our house?" Sandy asked.

"Sure, that sounds great!" Bryan answered, and Chad agreed.

Well, the supper was wonderful and after tidying everything up they all went into the twins' living room to relax after the incredibly strenuous day they'd all had. They were all quiet for a few minutes and then Sandy spoke up, "Hey Chad, I've heard you guys have dinner together many nights. What the dickens do you both talk about? Can you share your stories?"

"We talk about all the things we love—like nature! How'd you ladies like Gilpin Lake?"

"Oh, it was great! You are kidding again. Let's take a short break from the 'kidding contest'. Tell us what men like you talk about when they get together. We women want to know."

Bryan broke in, "In this great small town, there is so much going on that it seems we change the topic every night. Do you ladies like music, theater...sports?"

"Sports? That's what we thought you guys would be talking about. That's all most guys ever talk about. Even Albert Einstein used to watch the Broncos on TV."

Again, they all laughed.

"Actually," Chad commented, "we never talk about sports. Isn't that interesting, Bryan, we never talk about it or watch it. I guess because we are nerd scientists. And another thing we never talk about is politics, well, maybe the day before we vote we might mumble a little about who we think is the best guy."

"Or 'girl,'" Sandy shouted!

"Hey, Sandy, you didn't let me finish my sentence. I was going to say or girl, but I probably should have said girl or guy," Chad said.

They were having so much fun. Then Laura asked, "Alright, you don't talk about the forbidden topic, 'politics,' but how about the other forbidden topic, 'religion?'"

They all grew quiet.

"Well, actually we don't talk about religion, per se. But we have been talking about God. Bryan really is a strong believer in who we would call God, and I am sort of an agnostic who would like to believe but have doubts," Chad said.

Everyone cooled down.

"This is rather unbelievable," Sandy very quietly stated. "Laura and I are in the same place as you guys are. I'm absolutely positive God exists, is all around us and loves each one of us unconditionally. But Laura is in the same boat as you, Chad. She so wants to believe there is this loving God here, but she doubts there really is a Lord out there—or in here."

Bryan spoke out, "Holy cow, the good Lord must have brought the four of us all together to find the real answer."

Chad smiled and said, "Oh Bryan, can we say 'it's an interesting coincidence that brought us together.'"

"Chad loves the word 'coincidence,'" Bryan added.

Sandy jumped in with, "Oh my goodness, so does Laura like that word 'coincidence.' She thinks it could just be a coincidence that we have the right substance/texture of air to breathe surrounding our earth even after the earth was at one time on fire. Oh yeah, she feels that the water just happened to flood our planet after the earth's fire stopped. Where did air and water (H_2O) come from? Did it come from dust? How did we get here?"

"Wait," Bryan got up and added, "maybe we should hold off on our debates and watch "Saturday Night Live." I'm sure we could all agree, it's a really funny show."

They all cheered, and Bryan turned on the TV.

"You see," Chad argued, "It's got to be a coincidence that we all love 'Saturday Night Live' and we can watch it before we go to bed."

Halfway through the show they all dozed off as it had been one long day. At 11:30, Bryan woke up, turned off the TV and slipped out the front door leaving the rest of the gang in the twins' living room sleeping and snoring loudly.

Brian was so sleepy that he didn't notice the car parked across the street from the twins' house. The twins and Chad slept through the night, and because they did not wake up till morning, they didn't see the car with the guy in it shadowing Chad—and now Bryan, and Laura, and Sandy, too, because of their association with him. The bad guy left before dawn, so the friends were spared the terror of seeing him. The picture, however, was soon to change.

Gilpin Lake on the Zirkel Wilderness Trail.

Chapter X

It was mid October and the weather was getting colder. As often happens in Steamboat, several inches of snow covered the mountains and town. The buddies revved up their snow blowers and cleared their walks. Then they called Sandy and Laura at 8 o'clock in the morning to see if they needed help clearing their sidewalk.

"Darn, we both have to go to work early, so we can't do ours until we get home tonight," Laura confessed.

"Don't worry, we will come over and take care of everything. My first class isn't until 11:00," Bryan offered.

"Oh, you guys are real gentlemen. We will pay you back. Come over for supper tonight."

"We'll be there," Bryan assured Laura.

That night Sandy went out to sweep off the front porch steps before the buddies arrived. She noticed a car across the street with a guy in it. *I wonder what's going on*, she thought. Being a helpful person, she walked over to see if he needed anything. But before she got to the car, the driver sped off.

That's funny, she thought as she walked back to her front porch and put the broom away. She was very puzzled.

Fifteen minutes later, the buddies arrived and they hugged each other. While eating they got into an exciting discussion about the film they had recently seen and a character who had done a lot of bad things in his life, but gave great help to others in the end.

"Yeah," Sandy agreed. "All bad guys aren't bad all the time. Like that guy I saw across the street tonight just before you two arrived. He drove away when I walked over to see what he needed. That was rude. But maybe there's something I don't know that made him act that way."

There was silence. Chad looked at Bryan. Then they both looked away.

Finally, Chad spoke, "Ladies, dearest friends, I'm afraid there is something I have to tell you both. I'm ashamed of myself for not telling you sooner."

"Tell us what? You're a member of the Mafia and that gangster in the car wants to date me," Laura joked.

They all laughed. After they quieted down, Chad said, "No, it's serious. My work as a chemist involves analyzing drugs from a large pharmaceutical company that may be selling a product that has harmful effects on its users. After studying the products for three months, I have concluded that there is a chemical not listed in the ingredients which is incredibly addictive. We plan to file a lawsuit against this company soon. Bryan and I suspect someone from the board of the drug company, PPM, has employed this guy to shadow me, scare me and intimidate me so that I will not continue with my work. I should have told you both all about this because your friendship with me may be dangerous for you."

Laura said, "First of all, I don't think this person is just trying to scare you. I think he wants to do something much worse—eliminate you. So, the next step is not to end our friendship, but to call the police. Wake up! Why haven't you called the police already? Do men need a woman to get you their phone number?"

Bryan laughed, "No, I've got a phone book. It's just that we weren't sure what was going on, and most importantly, we don't want Chad's secret research to become part of the public record at this time."

"Okay," Chad spoke up, "Let's stay calm and wait until the next time he shows up, then we can decide what to do. I don't think this town has a big enough police force to guard our houses 24/7 even if we wanted them to. And, of course, the bad guy would never show up until the police left."

They all agreed, cleaned up, and played Scrabble until bedtime, which was a little later than usual because two of them were getting only vowels and two were getting only consonants.

Chapter XI

For several weeks the car with the guy didn't show up outside the buddies or the twins' homes. While cleaning up after Thanksgiving dinner at Chad's home, Bryan said, "Well, I guess we scared him away."

Sandy said, "No, I scared him away. You guys had nothing to do with it." Everyone laughed and went into the living room for their Scrabble game.

"Hey friends," Laura said, "can we have some interesting discussion instead of playing games tonight?"

Everyone sort of nodded their heads and sat down with their drinks on the sofa.

Chad started the conversation, "You know the Bible was written thousands of year ago. What makes Sandy and Bryan think something written so long ago is the truth today? What makes you think they got all of it right? What proof do we have that the stories in the Bible are accurate? Wasn't there a president who was said to have lied thousands of times, but because we had so many newspapers double checking that President's claims, we knew what was true and what was not. I don't think they had newspapers fact-check things 2000 years ago."

Sandy popped in with, "Chad, I'm wondering if you think there really was a Plato and an Aristotle?"

"Of course!"

"And do you think what we were told they said was true?"

"Of course."

"So, time doesn't raise any doubts for you about the accuracy of what we understand was passed down as their philosophies and what they did?"

"No, of course not."

"Well, I'm sure you are aware of the fact that the New Testament was written after Plato and Aristotle walked on this earth. This earth, which by coincidence," she said with tongue in cheek, "is kind of nice, has thousands of different plants, animals, birds, and rotates just at the right speed to give us six to twelve hours of darkness so we can go home from work and lie down and sleep without feeling guilty about not working?"

Everyone laughed.

"So, if we believe what was said over 2000 years ago, might it not be logical to believe what the writers of the Gospels related to us—which they wrote just a little later than 2000 years ago? Like 1,950 years ago. Actually, Paul wrote his letter to the Corinthians only 20 or so years later after what he describes and affirms as the Resurrection. And apparently there are other documents written at that time, like the Dead Sea Scrolls, which we have access to. And the Pyramids. When were they built? More than 4000 years ago. We don't doubt they were built by the Egyptians, do we? Whatever was passed along then has reached us today. Back then info was often passed along through conversation, and what witnesses said was usually considered reliable. We might not have Moses around anymore, but I think we know what he said and did. Also, when was Scrabble created? Let's play it now."

Chad ran over and grabbed the Scrabble box off the shelf and everybody sat around the dining room table getting ready to have fun and play their favorite game. They passed the bag with all the letters in it around to see who would go first. Everyone reached in and grabbed a letter with their eyes shut.

Bryan picked an 'A,' so he went first after everyone drew their seven letters.

Guess what? He was able to start with a seven-letter word, "Terrify," so he got fifty points for using all of his letters as well as double the word score for the value of the letters in "Terrify."

They were all absolutely amazed, or maybe they were all terrified at what Bryan was able to do. But they would soon be even more amazed with how the word that Bryan spelled was relevant to what was about to happen.

Sleeping Giant Mountain behind a hundred year old log cabin.

Chapter XII

As the game drew to a close, it looked like Bryan was going to win big time. Because everyone was having so much fun chatting about the incredible true "coincidence" that just occurred on the game board, they didn't hear the soft knock on the door.

After Chad put the game away and everyone hugged each other, the twins said their goodbyes. As Laura opened the front door, she noticed a piece of paper under the door. She picked it up and gave it to Chad because on the top was written "For Chad."

They rushed back into the living room, and Chad sat down and read: "Mr. Chad, I'm watching you every day."

They were shocked.

"Oh, now we must call the police to show them this letter. Perhaps it can be traced," Laura demanded.

Chad said, "Okay, now I will call the police, but I must tell you all who I trust with all my heart, I cannot disclose to anyone other than you all, the reason why I would be threatened by anyone. The pending lawsuit is about four weeks to completion and the law firm I am working with cannot let any information get out until the case is brought to court. Nothing about it can get in the paper or to the police. To be honest, how someone like this thug, who seems to be threatening me, could even find out about what I am doing, is a mystery to me. This has always been puzzling me. I wonder if there is someone in our law firm who is a spy and has warned the PPM Board what we are up to?"

Everyone was quiet as Chad picked up the phone to call the local police, but then he put the phone down.

"What is wrong?" Laura asked.

"Look at the paper," Chad responded.

What was left of it was disintegrating on the coffee table.

They were all shocked.

"Whoever is behind this understands chemistry. They obviously knew if what they left for me to see still existed when the police came, there would be a case against them if the paper could be traced. I'm afraid I don't have a case now."

Laura said, "Are you kidding? Sandy saw the car with that rat in it and we all will stick up for you."

Sandy spoke very calmly, "I've been praying a lot about this challenge we have. Let's try another approach. This whole thing is getting quite complicated. I'm moved to go along with what Pierre Pradervand puts forth in *The Gentle Art of Blessing*. Let's sit down, hold hands and pray about what to do next. Let's bless our enemy."

Chad asked, "Two of us are searching for God, and we still aren't sure God exists. I believe Jesus existed, but I don't believe he did all those miracles attributed to him."

Sandy asked, "Why did he become so famous in history if he didn't do all those incredible things. Isn't that why he became known all over the world?"

And Bryan added, "It puzzles me how the whole world doesn't doubt even for a second the truth Euclid taught us about geometry 300 BC. Yet some doubt what Jesus taught us about God 300 years later and the veracity of all the healings he did that are recorded in history by thousands of witnesses."

Chad said, "I don't know. I don't have an answer for that. But, how can we pray effectively if two of us are still unsure of God's existence? Though I like the idea of holding hands. Especially with you Sandy and Laura. Oh, yes and with my best buddy, too."

Everyone smiled and Sandy commented, "Well, God loves each of us and He really loves all those who care about each other—and we really do. I think banding together to ask for guidance will be a powerful prayer. Remember in Mark 9:24 Jesus said a father asked him to help his unbelief. Then Jesus healed the father's son even though the father was struggling with unbelief. I feel God will pour down guidance even if some of us are struggling with our unbelief."

"Sandy, you're incredible! With all your energy and joy, you sure make me feel cared for," Chad gratefully answered. "Let's pray."

They all sat around the dining room table and held hands. Sandy prayed, "Good Lord, help us to understand what we should do in this challenging situation. Help us to know that all things work together for good for those who love God. Help us to know that the drug company's real goal is to help mankind and they mean well. We pray they will listen for Thy voice and we pray that we will listen for Your voice too."

They were all quiet for a long time.

"Well, the message I'm getting," Bryan commented, "is to

hold off for the moment. But Chad you may be threatened more than we are, so what do you think?"

Chad was quiet with his eyes closed. Finally, he responded, "You all are 'So brave! So moral, So kind.' I'll wait to take any action."

Bryan went to the living room window and said, "It's snowing like crazy, but it's supposed to stop in the morning. Let's ski tomorrow. We have the day off. The champagne powder will be great."

They all cheered, and even Chad decided to take the morning off and get out on the slopes. They agreed to meet at 9:30 a.m. with the rest of the gang at the free shuttle stop at Seventh and Lincoln.

Path in the mountains close to Steamboat.

Chapter XIII

The next day, the friends took the shuttle to the gondola at the base of the mountain, put on their boots in the locker room and then hopped on the gondola for the ride to the top of Mt. Werner. When they all lined up at the top, Sandy, who at a beautiful five feet height, led the group straight down the slope. She was a fantastic skier and she took them down blues and then she raced into the woods.

"Oh, my goodness," the buddies shouted as they followed her. There was no way they could keep up with her so she, smiling behind her ski mask, waited at the edge of the forest. She looked over at a black slope she wanted to do next. Finally they all reached Sandy, although some of them had gently bumped into a couple of trees while going slowly through the woods.

"Are you kidding?" Bryan asked. "Now you are going to take us down this black slope? They're the hardest slopes on the mountain. Can't we take a little time to rest?"

"Alright, let's take that blue over there," Sandy pointed to an easier slope to the left of them.

As they casually crisscrossed down the mountain, an extremely aggressive snowboarder raced down behind them. Chad did not realize the boarder was behind him and turned into the boarder's path. He was hit by the guy who was probably going over thirty miles an hour. Chad was hurled into the air and fell a good ten feet down the mountain. The others were in front of Chad so they didn't see it happen.

Chad was quite bruised, but by the grace of God, he wasn't seriously injured in any bad way. The boarder stopped and came over to help Chad get up and apologized. He asked, "Man, are you alright?"

"I'm fine. Thank you for checking on me."

"I don't want to lecture you, but with so many snowboarders on the mountain, you've got to glance around before your turns to see what's coming around the bend!" the snowboarder advised.

"You're right. I thank God I'm alright. Oh my gosh, I'm starting to bring God into the picture."

The two of them parted in a friendly manner, and Chad slowly continued down the mountain.

At the base, the rest of the gang was waiting for Chad, and they all yelled with joy because he looked okay when they skied over to him.

"Are you alright? What happened to you?" Bryan asked.

"Yeah, I'm fine. Got hit by a snowboarder and tossed in the air and landed ten feet down the mountain. By the grace of God, I'm alright."

"Hey, what's going on here. You just brought God into the picture?" Sandy exclaimed.

Chad laughed and said, "I guess I'm hanging around too much with you and Bryan."

Laura spoke up, "Is it possible this guy was that thug who has been shadowing you?"

"No, he came over and apologized and helped me up. He didn't have a mask on so I could see his face. I'm sure if he was that bad guy he would not have stopped, and he would have had a mask on to hide his face so I couldn't have identified him."

Again, everyone was grateful that the morning was going to end well, and they went to the locker room to put away their skis and headed back to town for lunch.

And it was a great lunch at Noodles and More and… they didn't talk politics. They talked about the wonderful coincidence that occurred: the snow was perfect "champagne" powder, the sun was just perfect, and the angle of the slopes was great, and the gravity was just right. They were delighted the earth was not twirling any faster.

Skiing down a Blue Slope on Mt. Werner.

Chapter XIV

On Monday Chad was winding up the research for his chemical analysis of the many products PPM was selling. The law firm was grateful for the work he had done and very soon they were going to file the lawsuit against the giant drug company.

On one of Chad's calls and discussions with lawyers at the firm, he let them know about what appeared to be a plan for a man to frighten him and get him to stop his research—research that would threaten PPM's reputation. Chad wondered how anyone learned what he was doing. Was it possible there was a leak from the firm?

The lawyers were shocked and were totally convinced that no one from their firm was ratting on Chad.

"Is your research regarding PPM's products stored anywhere someone might have access to?" asked Dimitry, the head of the law firm when brought into the conversation.

"It's all on my computer, and I have not let anyone have access since I started this project."

"When you are not at home, what do you do with the computer?"

"I lock it up in a closet. I don't take the chance of someone breaking in and stealing it."

Dimitry instructed Chad, "There is one possibility that seems to be occurring in this incredible age of technology. People are hacking into computers online everyday hoping to get some information that's going to make them money. It's possible this is what happened. It might be too late to save the show, but I suggest you print two copies of all you have done and give one to us and keep your copy secure. Then destroy everything that is on your computer relating to our project. From now on, print everything out each day and then delete what you did and don't send us information about it in emails."

"I'll do that, but before I destroy the electronic data from the hard drive of my computer, I'll copy it onto a 'flash drive' and store the thumb drive in a safe deposit box."

After Chad got back at work, he immediately printed everything out, copied it onto a flash drive and then removed from his hard drive, all that he had amassed in the last four months.

The next day he got an email from an unknown source that said, "I have all your info. It's too late to stop me."

Chad was blown away. He quickly tried to answer the email to trace the address, but it wouldn't receive. He called Bryan and explained what had just happened. He asked if he knew a computer expert at the college.

Bryan was on a lunch break and responded that one of the students in his class was a computer genius. He'd see if he could help Chad.

Around 5:00 p.m. there was a knock on Chad's door and it turned out to be Michael Smith, the computer genius Bryan spoke of.

After Michael checked everything out, he told Chad the email address was no longer valid. Obviously it had just been temporarily active and had been immediately deleted. He was sorry to tell Chad there was no way to trace it now.

Later that night the friends got together for supper at the twins' home, and Chad shared with everyone what an unpleasant day it had been for him.

"If God is here, I wish He would help me out of this mess. Sandy, do you think He's not helping me because I don't believe in Him?"

Sandy answered, "I feel God helps us all—even the unbelievers. I feel He is Love and He Loves us all unconditionally. My feeling is that He's helping you right now. In fact, He will help everyone. I think we have to be patient. There has got to be a solution to all this, but we can't outline what the solution is or think it's going to be a coincidence. In the end, I think all will be blessed."

"Wow, Sandy," Chad chuckled.

"Your thoughts inspire me," Bryan with his usual humility commented.

Then Chad said, "Well, if whoever is threatening me stops his stupid acts and something works out with PPM, maybe I'll start believing in God."

Sandy said, "You must be kidding! I don't think you can bribe God."

And everyone laughed and then they set up the Scrabble board on the coffee table and enjoyed another evening together. They had no idea what amazing thing was going to happen the next day.

Beautiful snow.

Chapter XV

All the news stations broadcast the next day that PPM announced certain ingredients in their products had an addictive chemical that the Board of Directors and executives did not realize were part of their product. They said they were changing the formulas immediately and were refunding anyone who wished to return their products.

Bryan rushed over to Chad's house with the news that Chad had not heard because he had been working in his lab.

When Chad heard the news, he immediately called the law firm to find out what the plan was now.

Dmitry responded, "We aren't sure. We could still sue PPM, but it's possible what just happened might be a better solution than going to trial. Buyers are getting their money back, and the truth is out. It would cost a fortune to fight this case in court. I don't think it would be worthwhile for our small group of clients to fight for more than they will be getting from PPM's voluntary payout. It would cost the clients more than they would get, even if we won the case.

PPM has so much money they could drag it on forever. I feel we should just be happy with what's finally happened."

That night the friends got together and were so excited about all that had happened.

"Wow, Sandy, I wonder if it is just a coincidence, or did God work it out for everyone?" Chad asked humbly. "Actually— we aren't out of the woods yet, because this afternoon I got a call from that nut who's been stalking me. It had no caller ID and I foolishly answered it. He said, 'Chad, you may think things have been worked out for you, but they haven't. After I hacked into your computer and found out what you were doing, I got in touch with a board member of PPM and told him what was going on. So I got him or her, I won't mention their name, to secretly pay me to stalk you and get you to stop your work. Your work was going to hurt PPM. So, someone on their Board was secretly paying me to stalk you and get you to stop. Well, now I'm not making any more money because your research convinced PPM to compromise, and that means I'm out of work. So, you are going to pay for this!! Goodbye.'"

"So, Sandy, Laura and Bryan, you see why we still have a threat?" Chad declared.

This gave them a lot to think about as they went to their homes.

Chapter XVI

The next morning about 8 o'clock Bryan ran over to Chad's house and knocked on the door. To his surprise, Sandy and Laura walked up, too. Bryan turned around, "Hey what are you two wonderful ladies doing here?"

Sandy answered, "We have a great idea that can help Chad relax."

"Ha, so do I! I bet my idea is better than yours," Bryan bragged.

"Really? We are going to suggest that Chad install a video doorbell camera so he can always see who is on the porch," Laura stated.

"Stop it, are you kidding? That's exactly what I am suggesting," answered Bryan.

"No, Bryan, you are kidding. This camera would make a video record so Chad can use it for evidence."

Then Chad came out the front door. "Hi, everyone! I knew you were knocking because the video camera I bought last night showed me nothing but friends on my front porch."

Everyone but Chad burst out laughing.

"Chad, are you kidding? That was exactly what we were going to suggest you buy."

"Yes, I'm kidding. I didn't get it yet, but I plan to, and something told me you all were going to come over and bug me. See, I'm not so dumb."

They all hugged and then left for work. Chad took time off to purchase a great camera and set it up. It was very small on the doorbell so someone at the front door might not notice it. It worked really well, and his friends came over that night to check it out. They all agreed it was very effective. But they gave it the supreme test by ordering pizza for supper and then when the doorbell rang, they all rushed over to the image on Chad's cell phone to check it out. Yes, it was the pizza guy, so they opened the door. Then they sat down and enjoyed the pizza and the salad the ladies had brought.

"Everyone, tomorrow is Saturday. Why don't we go to Lake Catamont and cross-country ski on the lake because I hear it's frozen solid with a lot of snow on it," Sandy suggested.

"Sure. What time do you want to meet and where?" Chad asked.

"9:30 at our house and we will drive," Laura said.

They said good-bye and went their ways to get a good night's sleep. Laura, Sandy and Bryan found themselves contemplating about whether they, too, should get video cameras.

A place to walk near Rabbit Ears Pass.

Chapter XVII

The next morning, they rushed to Walmart to get their doorbell video cameras and when they arrived back at the twins' house, Chad was on their front porch.

"So sorry Chad, but we went to get our cameras."

"No problem, I was just enjoying the cold weather."

They all laughed because it was about 5 degrees below zero. "How could you be saying that?"

They all packed into the twins' car and drove off to beautiful Lake Catamount.

When they got there, the sun came out and the temperature went up to 38. In beautiful Steamboat with its very dry air, that wasn't bad at all.

They had so much fun. They raced around the lake on their skis and enjoyed the lovely mountain scenery surrounding the lake.

On their second time around the lake about 11:00 a.m., they noticed a guy skiing by himself about 100 yards behind them.

They paused and turned to face him. He was too far away for them to get a good look at him and he was wearing a face mask. Once he saw the friends had stopped skiing and were looking in his direction, he turned around, took off his skis, and ran off the trail and disappeared behind the ski rental building.

"Do you think that guy was following us?" Laura asked. They all got goose bumps, but it wasn't the cold weather that caused it.

Chapter XVIII

They quickly finished the last turn around Lake Catamount, packed up their cross-country skis, and drove to the Haymaker Restaurant for lunch.

Chad was the first to start the conversation, "I am so sorry I've brought you all into this mess."

Laura, who always seemed to care for everyone, responded with, "Chad, I'm not sure why this has happened, but I want you to know that I am grateful to be in a position to support a great guy like you. I'm not sure why I have this feeling, but it's one of great joy to be with you and support you in this really challenging situation. I'm not sure I believe in God, but if I did, I'd say She brought us all together so we could support each other and you, Chad, in your journey to stand up for the moral right. Look what's already happened. Those drugs coming from PPM are no longer going to contain addictive ingredients and thousands, maybe millions of dollars have been saved by the cancelled lawsuits."

Sandy and Bryan agreed with Laura. They all held hands and Chad, who had tears in his eyes said, "Okay, let's talk about something else. I'm so touched that you are sticking with me, but maybe if we talk about something else, we will relax a little."

"Politics?" Bryan joked.

"Sure," Sandy agreed, "I'm voting for Lincoln. Who are you all voting for?"

"Washington is my pick," Bryan quipped.

"I really like Teddy Roosevelt," Laura butted in.

"You've got my vote, Laura, but could we call him Chaddy Roosevelt, like me?"

After laughing so loud that the other patrons in the restaurant were staring at them, they paid their bills, hopped in the twins' car and headed back to town.

"Why don't you guys come on in and we can continue our political conversation," Sandy suggested. As you can guess, that wasn't going to turn out to be the topic of discussion.

Brown now, but soon will be white.

Chapter XIX

"Wow, how do the two of you keep your place so neat and clean?" Bryan asked.

"Because we are girls," the twins shouted in unison.

"Well, Chad's not a girl and his place is neater than yours—sometimes."

"Occasionally," Sandy joked.

The girls poured lemonade and set out an avocado dip with crackers, and they settled on the two sofas facing each other. Then there was a knock on the door. They froze and then looked at the video screen on Laura's phone. It was the twins' neighbors, Margie and Ken Dodd. Margie was holding a bouquet of flowers.

The friends sighed a great relief, smiled and opened the door.

"Hi, Sandy. We've heard that you play Scrabble! We do, too, and we wondered if we could join you?" the Dodds asked.

Sandy smiled and said, "Absolutely, we would love to have you join us. But, can we schedule another time? We are just about to have a meaningful discussion."

"Sure, we just wanted to let you know we'd love to join you anytime. And here are some flowers I was given for my birthday a couple days ago. I think they still are beautiful and we are going out-of-town for a few days, and I hate to see these lovely flowers go to waste. So, I thought you ladies would enjoy them." Then they turned and waved good-bye.

"Oh, thank you Margie and Ken! We will see you soon for Scrabble," Laura shouted. "And happy birthday to you, Margie."

As the friends returned to the living room and slumped down on the sofas, Bryan stated, "What an incredible day. Cross country skiing on new snow on a sunny day in one of the most glorious places on earth, a great lunch, and a visit from your neighbors who brought us a gift of beautiful flowers. And now we can relax and talk about God who made all this possible."

Chad asked, "You all don't think it was just coincidence?" as he smiled.

"Well, Chad, you know how Bryan and I feel about 'coincidences,' but I'd like to get your opinion on some questions," Sandy playfully answered.

"Go to it," Chad replied.

"If the sperm is the cause of the creation of man and woman, where did the first sperm come from?" Sandy asked.

"Maybe from the first man?" Chad quipped.

"Then how did the first man get here?"

"Maybe he evolved from the ape?"

"Where did the first ape come from?"

"Maybe he evolved from the fungus in the sea," they all chuckled.

Then Sandy said, "How did the fungus get here?"

"Ha, how far are you going to go back? Maybe it all came from the moon," Chad suggested.

Sandy asked, "Are you kidding? How did it get there? And what came first—the earth or the moon?"

Now they were all laughing.

Sandy continued, "Doesn't it puzzle you a little where all this came from?"

Chad joked, "Maybe there were a lot of 'coincidences' happening. No, I'm not puzzled. I'm dumb-founded."

Sandy kept asking, "Doesn't it amaze you that from that sperm, that tiny little drop of liquid, we grow into a body with two eyes, two ears, two legs, two arms and lungs and blood vessels and hearts and some things I won't mention in front of you all." They all laughed at her humor.

Bryan jumped in with, "And isn't it amazing the sperm has enough intelligence in it to teach us how to smile when we are babies?" More chuckles. "And did that sperm have it all figured out that Beethoven was going to be one of the greatest composers ever. Oh, and that John Denver was going to be one of the greatest folk singers of our time? And which sperm contained Leonard Bernstein's 'West Side Story?'"

Then Chad jumped in with, "Come on, let's get serious. They have done studies and examined the details of the sperm, and they found incredible energy and numbers of particles in the contents that, I guess, directs the creation of the human species once it unites with the egg safely inside the woman."

Sandy questioned, "Okay, Chad, how did all that stuff get into the sperm and the woman's egg and how did the first sperm get created with all its details? Who created it?"

Chad answered, "Maybe it evolved from dust or something."

"Are you kidding? Can you tell me how the dust had enough intelligence to evolve into a sperm?" asked Sandy. "And how did the sperm get into the first man? And we need a man to insert sperm into a woman, so was the first man, or ape created without the sperm? Doesn't all this make you ponder our current theories about creation? Or did this sperm lying in the dust create a man after the dust created the sperm without a woman's help? And then did the woman say to the man, 'Give me your sperm and I'll create a man from it.' Oh, yes, and what language were they speaking?" They all laughed.

Sandy went on, "And then did dust say, 'Hey, don't you need me to create sperm anymore?'

"Actually, there are so many scientists and writers who are beginning to look at our so-called world from a different perspective. The emergence of the theory of quantum physics has opened a whole new ball game. A great scientist, Peter Russell, who originally was an atheist, wrote an incredible book called *From Science to God* which sees the truth of our existence in our consciousness, not in all the material we seem to be observing. The neurosurgeon, Eben Alexander, M.D., reaches similar conclusions in his book *The Map of Heaven*."

At this point Bryan jumps in, "Well Sandy, you have done a lot of research."

"I guess I have. Besides the Bible, I read lots of books by scientists who have approached the spiritual world," Sandy replied.

Sandy just couldn't resist ending the discussion with, "Maybe creation is just a thousand 'coincidences' or maybe it's what Job said in Job 33:4: 'The spirit of God hath made me, and the breath of the Almighty hath given me life.'"

They all hugged each other and said their good-byes.

Moose may live in Steamboat, but don't get to vote.

Chapter XX

The next day was Sunday and Bryan called the twins and Chad and suggested they join him on a forty-five-minute drive to Clark to view the wonderful scenery with the tons of beautiful white snow covering the valley. The three feet of snow didn't seem to discourage the cattle and horses from making paths out in the fields to feed on the big hay bales the farmers put out for them.

As they drove toward Clark, Laura suggested, "Oh, this is so beautiful, let's go past Clark to Glen Eden and go to that good restaurant up there."

"That's exactly what I was going to suggest as soon as I sensed you were hungry," Bryan joked.

They agreed and soon found themselves at Glen Eden, parking the car and quickly running into the restaurant because it had started to snow again, hard.

"Gosh, this snow scares me. Do you think we can make it back home with all the snow on the road?" Chad asked. They looked a little glum, but Bryan reassured them everything was going to be all right because he had good snow tires. That raised everyone's spirits. The food was good, but they decided not to stay too long.

As they began driving slowly on the snow-covered road, they noticed another car was right behind them. Bryan was uncomfortable with the follower, so when he found a place where he could pull over, he let that car pass him. The "follower" passed him and then disappeared in the snowstorm. About four miles down the road, they passed a car in a driveway that looked just like the one that had been behind them earlier. After they passed the car, Chad and Sandy looked behind them and saw the car pull out and head in their direction. This made them all nervous.

Bryan picked up his speed after he got around a curve. The follower sped up, too, but was going too fast entering the curve and ended up sliding off the road and getting stuck in a shallow ditch.

Chad was watching all this out the back window, and he let everyone know what happened.

Bryan slowed down immediately, and everyone sighed a sigh of relief.

"When we get back in cell phone range, I'll call AAA and tell them what just happened. I'll offer to pay for the service for that driver, and maybe we can find out his name and track him down," Bryan informed the twins and Chad.

"So, Bryan you are convinced that the driver is the guy who has been haunting Chad?" Laura asked.

"He could be," Bryan replied.

After a few miles Bryan made the call and asked if the AAA would give them the name of the person they helped.

When they were safely home, Bryan got a call from AAA. They said that Suzy Patrich was so grateful for Bryan's generous offer to help her, that she wanted to invite him for supper to repay him. She apologized for driving so close to him, but she foolishly had left her phone at home and wanted to stay close to him in case something went wrong while she was driving on the treacherous road—which is exactly what had occurred.

Bryan called his friends and told them what happened, and they all responded with, "Bryan, you must be kidding."

Hahn's Peak close to Glen Eden.

Chapter XXI

At Christmas the twins and the buddies brought their families to town for the festivities. They put them up in their homes and at the college dorms that were empty for the Christmas vacation. Since the twins' home was the largest, they selected it to be the place to get twenty-two people together, and it was quite a ball.

After Christmas vacation, the friends found themselves working so hard for the next week that no Scrabble, discussions, suppers or trips in the countryside were possible for them. Laura had to teach all day, and at night she had many papers to grade. Sandy was involved in several new law cases, and she spent her nights writing an article on immigration Harvard had asked for. Chad was involved writing articles about his new techniques for analyzing drug contents requested by a state authority. And Bryan was tied up teaching and grading papers and tests as they headed for the end of the semester.

Then it happened. They all had a break at the same time. Chad called it a "coincidence," Bryan the "Grace of God," Laura "luck" and Sandy called it "gratitude."

Sandy asked, "What else could you say when all your friends who you haven't seen for a week and who you love doing things with are free to spend some time together again?"

Sandy called the buddies and suggested, "Hey, how about taking a drive Saturday to Meeker and see where that famous Meeker Massacre occurred, where all those Ute Indians were horribly killed. We could honor those Indians and the the drive would be gorgeous, and the snow isn't too bad. We have snow tires, so I think we would be safe for the five-hour round trip."

They all thought it was a great idea and planned to meet at 9:00 a.m.

It would turn out to be a very exciting journey.

Chapter XXII

As the twins pulled up to Bryan's and Chad's homes, Sandy honked her horn. The buddies ran out to Sandy's car with giant smiles on their faces, happy they were finally able to get together again to enjoy the lovely Colorado scenery on a sunny winter day.

At first, they drove through the little town of Phippsburg and then went up to Dunkley Pass, taking in all the spectacular scenery on the drive. They parked at the top of the pass and trod through the snow to the edge of a cliff to look down on the valley and see the beautiful Flat Top Mountains in the distance encased in many feet of gorgeous snow.

"Oh, my goodness, this is so so beautiful," Sandy exclaimed. "Is this just a coincidence Chad and Laura, or did the good Lord have something to do with what we are beholding?"

Chad answered, "However this got here, it's sure incredible! And, to share this with my dear friends makes this a joy I will never forget."

They took dozens of pictures with their phone cameras

and then stomped through the snow back to the car. Then they learned the highway to Meeker was closed because of the snow. So, they returned back to Phippsburg. They were shocked when a huge herd of elk suddenly rushed across the road in front of the car. Sandy tried desperately to slow down, but she couldn't stop in time and the car went right through the center of the herd without touching any animal. As they sped through the herd, they could see the faces of the elk out the right window and the rears of these wild animals out the left window.

When they realized no animal was hurt and their car wasn't damaged, they screamed with joy and pulled over to the side of the road. They had just avoided what might have been a terrible catastrophe. "How on earth did that space occur just as we reached the elk herd?" Chad said.

"Oh, was that a 'coincidence,' or was God looking out for us?" Sandy asked. They all quietly pondered the event as they started to drive back down the mountain.

No one said anything for several minutes as they drove to Oak Creek, a little village on their way back to Steamboat. Finally, as they approached the little town, Laura said, "Not to disturb you, as I assume you are all contemplating what just happened, but I wonder if you buddies have heard about the the woman who was the famous former mayor who ran Oak Creek for three terms?"

"No, why is she famous?" Bryan asked.

"Because she did so much good for this little town. She was a hippie. She was someone you never would have thought would become a mayor of any town. Her name was Cargo Rodeman. The 'Cargo' name came from the fact that as a child she was shipped around the country. She went through a lot of difficult times in her life, but she never let adversities stop her visions for helping others. Despite years of many personal challenges, and after seeing many serious abuses of power in her town, she decided to run for mayor of Oak Creek. She felt she wanted to help the town make some changes that would, in the end, benefit everyone. If she could help her little town straighten out a lot of things that needed change, this would give her great joy. Apparently, the police department was corrupt, and she fixed that. She got the town a state-of-the-art water treatment plant by raising the money needed. That's just a couple things and whenever she spoke at the City Council, you'd think she was a graduate of Harvard. I want to write a book about her.

"I just brought this up so you could enjoy what you see as we drive through the cute little town. It's an important part of America, as so many other little towns are. There must be hundreds of little towns all over the country that have interesting stories like this one about how they have survived and grown," Laura stated.

Chad added, "This is what America is all about."

"Small towns?" Bryan asked jokingly, and then continued, "No, I think it's about the persistence of good morality even in small towns. In fact, I bet morality coming from small towns can 'trickle up' to the big towns, even Washington, D.C."

They all shouted, "I hope so!"

Then Sandy said, "Hey, let's change that to 'We know so!'" They laughed and poked and patted each other as they drove out of Oak Creek and headed for Steamboat.

Too bad the bad guy shadowing Chad didn't seem to understand morality. He did, however, understand the meaning of the word "persistence," and he was sure if he persisted, he could enjoy the word "revenge."

The elk getting ready to run across the road.

Chapter XXIII

The winter was filled with joy for the twins and the buddies. They skied, snow-shoed, went to the hot springs up on the mountain, attended Steamboat Springs Symphony Orchestra concerts, perused all of the fifteen art galleries on the First Friday Art Walks, visited the Tread of Pioneers museum, had dinner together and of course played Scrabble when they could find free time in their really busy schedules.

As the winter played out, the friends started to look forward to spring when they could get back to hiking, river rafting, biking, horseback riding, ballooning, sailing and canoeing on Steamboat Lake and the Stagecoach Reservoir.

Around May, the snow stopped and that was just fine with them. But what they were most grateful for was the fact that the past winter the guy who was threatening Chad seemed to have ceased his threats. Was that because of the cold weather? Maybe. Maybe not. Was he still around?

"Did he finally become a good boy?" asked Bryan.

Chad replied, "Are you kidding? I bet he is as angry as

ever and may be putting together a plan to finish me off...
as well as my friends."

Sandy lovingly spoke, "Come on Chad. Everything is going to be all right."

One night when alone, Chad asked Bryan if he felt the same incredible joy that a coincidence had brought the lovely ladies into their lives to enjoy the world together.

Bryan replied, "Are you kidding? I think the good Lord brought us all together to support each other and feel what happiness is being poured on His children."

Chad said, "Well, whatever the cause of this gift we have, it sure is fun. Bryan, these two girls are really lovely. Have you ever thought of ah...ah...of getting a little closer to one of them?"

Bryan quickly responded, "That's a tough question." And it was going to take a while before the whole truth would be revealed.

Chapter XXIV

Both Chad and Bryan went to bed that night thinking about Chad's question that Bryan couldn't answer. They both had had several romantic relationships in the past which almost worked out but unfortunately didn't. Bryan lost his dearest love to a tragic car accident three years earlier and Chad had, at two different times, loved ones who couldn't put up with his work schedule—or maybe, it was more the fact that in spite of his taking off time to be with them, they felt his real love was for his projects, not them.

The next afternoon after Chad put his workload on the shelf, he walked over to Bryan's place, opened the door and called, "Bryan, are you back yet from teaching?" No answer. He walked around to Bryan's back yard and there was Bryan working on his garden, getting it ready for spring planting. "Oh, there you are."

"Yeah, I've got to get these tomato plants in my garden. What's up?"

"Well, I wondered if you had any thoughts about the question I asked you last night?" Smiling, he said, "I wondered if you could answer the question before we go over to the twins' for supper tonight."

"Ha, ha—that makes sense. But don't you dare think you can put me on the spot now, because I'm going to put you on the spot first. Have you, Chad, ever thought about getting a little closer to one of them?" and Bryan burst out laughing.

"Bryan, you're a riot. Yes, I did, but then I couldn't decide which one I should give the 'romantic box' to since they are both great women. Then I paused and thought, why do I need to pull out the 'romantic box' anyway? What we've got going is fantastic. Let's not spoil it with the romantic game, yet."

"Chad, are you kidding? That's exactly what I was thinking. It's such a gift the four of us have been given. Our 'Friends Club' seems just to be filled with mutual love, kindness, respect, and joy. You couldn't ask for anything better. We seem to be able to subdue our personalities and put each friend, and I mean each one, before ourselves. It's an incredible opportunity for us to find that all of us are so compatible. Maybe down the road I can answer your question."

Chad replied, "Hey, are you kidding? That's also the way I was thinking. Oh, not to change the subject, Bryan, did you start the meat loaf we're serving the twins tonight?"

"Oh, gosh!" Bryan ran inside to get it started. He only had one hour to complete the task.

Now as it happened, while getting the salads and desserts ready for the game night, the twins were having a similar discussion to the one the buddies had just finished.

"Don't you look forward to this evening with those great guys?" Laura commented.

"Sure, I love to spend quality time with men who treat woman with respect," Sandy affirmed.

Sandy went on, "Yes, I sure do. They are both wonderful men—kind, thoughtful and good athletes who are almost as good as us, ha. I think Bryan could almost catch up to me when we were skiing this winter."

"Sis, I bet you were slowing down because you didn't want him to feel bad," Laura joked.

"And they are good looking, too, Sandy added. "That was a problem for me because, as men and women often unfortunately do, I thought 'wow' these guys sure are good looking, which one do I want? Then, I woke up and realized that was not a practical journey to take, yet. We are having such a great time as a harmonious gang, let's not confuse things now. We should enjoy the glorious situation the way it is. Let's not mess things up quite yet."

Laura agreed, "You must be kidding—that's exactly how I look at things."

Then there was knock on the door. Sandy yelled, "Come on in!" and the party got started. And no one was going to reveal who their favorite Scrabble player was. Self-interest was not on the table. Brotherly and sisterly love had taken charge. But more was to come down the road.

Flat Top Mountains near Steamboat.

Chapter XXV

When the twins straightened everything up that night, they sat and chatted for a few moments before turning in.

"One of the things that really touches me about the buddies is that I always feel very safe with them," Laura mentioned.

"Yes," Sandy replied. "They probably don't realize that both of us have had some tough experiences with some men in the past." Most men really don't know what it's like to be a woman. What it's like to have to walk alone in Chicago, getting off the subway in the dark, and walking to your apartment. We never knew if we were going to make it back home without being attacked by some crazy guy who wanted to conquer a lady. Men don't have to carry pepper spray with them as they walk through the city. At least that's not the first thing they put in their pockets before their keys. I guess we are so grateful that we feel so safe with Chad and Bryan."

"Right," Sandy said. "Now, let's get a good night's sleep and see what tomorrow has in store for us."

They were going to need all the rest they could get because they were going to have quite a taxing day ahead of them, and it was going to be a little frightening.

Chapter XXVI

Sandy called Bryan early on a Saturday morning in late June and asked, "How would you both like to go bike through California Park today? The wildflowers are going to be spectacular. I don't think there will be any bears there, but don't count on my prediction being very accurate. Just to be on the safe side, let's take the bear spray along."

"Sounds like a wonderful idea. I'll call Chad and see what he thinks."

Chad was excited to join the expedition and asked, "Can we use your car, Bryan? I think that bike extension on the rear of your big Ford Escape and the bike racks on the roof would save us driving two cars."

"Sure, see ya over here at 9:30."

After getting the bikes secured, the friends hopped into Bryan's big van and off they went from Steamboat to the edge of California Park in little more than an hour. The fields were glorious and were covered with spectacular wildflowers of purple, yellow and white. And the brilliant red Indian Paint Brush were amassed right next to the road.

Sandy asked Chad, "Isn't it wonderful that flowers, who come from dust, have the intelligence to have these different colors in the five, eight or ten petals?"

Chad joked, "It's just a nice coincidence that each species decides on their exact color to keep as their own and exactly the right number of petals they can put forward. If they get greedy and slip in an extra petal, they are punished by the dust, who is the boss."

As usual, the friends spent a lot of their journey laughing.

When they got to the base of the park, they pulled over to the side of the road and parked.

They got the bikes off the van and, as usual, Sandy took off as the leader.

"Oh, this is great!" Laura yelled, "but watch out for the bears."

Sandy yelled back, "Don't worry, I've got the bear spray in my pack and I'll shoo them away if they want to intrude on our party."

After two hours of wonderful biking through the valley-like terrain surrounded by lovely mountains, the group headed back to Bryan's van. As usual, Sandy got back first and after getting her bike installed on one of the bike racks, she stood up and waved to the rest of the gang as they approached her.

Laura, the last biker, was pretty far in the rear and Sandy realized that there was some animal running right next to her. It was staying at her side, but obviously Laura didn't notice it yet. Then she did. She screamed and started to pedal faster than she ever had in her life. That didn't seem to impress the mountain lion, and it had no problem keeping up with her. The rest of the team were now off their bikes and standing by the car and watching the race with horror.

Both Laura and the lion approached the group head on, and they all raised their arms and started screaming. The lion stopped and Laura kept going, still screaming, and rode right up to Bryan and fell off the bike into his arms. Everybody kept yelling and screaming, but that didn't seem to impress the beautiful creature. At about ten yards away, it sat down and stared at them. Everybody calmed down. They stared back. The big cat started to lick itself.

"What is going on here?" Chad asked.

Bryan answered, "I think he just wanted to join the party and we aren't being too welcoming. Let's all walk slowly over toward him and see what happens."

"You must be kidding, Bryan" Laura stated.

"Laura, I'll hold your hand—come on, and Sandy has the bear spray if needed," Bryan assured her.

So, believe it or not, they started to walk slowly toward the guy with a big mouth and a lot of beautiful teeth.

That did it. The lion said good-bye and turned around and sprinted off.

"Thank you, Lord, for this incredible experience," Sandy cried out.

Laura commented, "It's getting hard to think all of this was just a coincidence, but whatever it was, I'll remember it for the rest of my life."

"Hey, Chad, maybe it was that guy who threatened you that hired the mountain lion to scare us," Bryan joked.

Chad answered, "I don't think he can speak lion language."

They loaded up their bikes and headed back to Steamboat. What a day. And more was to come.

Spring flowers in the mountains with the
Rabbit Ears' giant rocks in the distance.

Chapter XXVII

To end the perfect day, the friends got together for a potluck supper and then their usual Scrabble game. Later, as everyone said good-bye, Sandy suggested, "Why don't we tube down the Yampa River tomorrow after we attend church? The river is flowing big time because of the snow this winter."

Chad asked, "I've never done that. Is it dangerous?"

"Not too much. Can you swim, Chad?"

"Yes, but I'm not sure I'd like to swim in that cold, or I should say freezing snow-melt, water."

"Chad, it's not dangerous, but a lot of fun. The only time you could get really wet is if you get discombobulated while going over the little falls. Are we on?"

"Sure!" everyone agreed.

Sandy asked, "Why don't we meet at our house after church at 1:00, take two cars and rent four tubes in town. Then we can park one of the cars by the Community Center where we'll be able to get out of the river at the end of our tubing journey. Then, we can all get in one car and drive past the Rabbit Ears Motel where we can put our tubes in the river and start to float."

"Sounds like a great plan," everyone spoke out and then they said their good-byes.

Before heading to bed Laura exclaimed, "Wow, you can talk these guys into anything!"

"Oh, I just hope they don't end up getting too wet."

Chapter XXVIII

Everything seemed to be working out nicely on Sunday. Bryan and Sandy went to their separate churches; Laura joined Bryan and Chad went along with Sandy. As is often the case, non-believers sometimes enjoy church services in spite of their non-belief.

After lunch together at Freshies, they rented tubes and set out on their journey. Things were going well and they enjoyed the beautiful scenery while racing each other down the rushing river. Chad began to build his confidence as he maneuvered the first little falls. Since Chad had never done anything like this before, it was understandable that the falls seemed a little threatening. But he kept gaining more and more confidence as he successfully went over each of the little falls.

"We are almost finished, Chad, and you've done great. The next one is the biggest one and it's by our great library. You'll also see some hot springs flowing off to the left just before you get to it. Smell the Sulphur?" Sandy shouted at Chad.

She probably should have kept quiet. Chad was

distracted by what Sandy was saying and looked at the huge rocks where the hot springs burst out, so he didn't realize what was happening to his tube. It turned around and all of a sudden, he found himself going backwards down the falls.

"Oh, no!" he yelled, and before he knew it, he had turned over. He found himself under the tube and struggling to get out. Soon the water calmed down as he was swept down the river, and lo and behold, he came to the surface. And there were his friends surrounding him, stretching out their hands to grab him and pull him back into his tube Bryan had grabbed.

They pulled over to the riverbank where their car was parked by the Community Center. But poor Chad was soaked and chilled.

"Chad, could you walk back up the river? If you get in my car you will soak it," Bryan said.

"Oh, I hope you are kidding," Chad responded with teeth chattering, and they all laughed.

Bryan had brought some towels to sit on, and Chad soon stopped shivering when Bryan turned on the car's heater.

That night after their Scrabble game Chad commented as he left for home, "This was a great day and you know what the best thing is?"

"No," everyone answered.

"I don't have to take a bath tonight. I already took one in the river. It was great, but I wish they could have turned up the heat a little."

Tubers that made it over the falls.

Chapter XXIX

Well, the summer was turning out to be a fantastic time for the twins and buddies. Steamboat is a wonderful place to take a vacation, but if you live there full-time, it can be even better. Mountains covered with an infinite variety of beautiful spring flowers, forests of spectacular fall leaves of all colors, music, theater, balloon rides above the picturesque city, chances to watch cowboys riding bulls at the rodeo, river tubing and rafting.

What is there not to like? Oh, I forgot to mention—you might get eight or nine months of snow. And sometimes the very top of the mountains never get rid of that white stuff.

But this didn't seem to bother the friends and even though their recent summer and fall were so much fun, they couldn't wait for the ski season to arrive. The guys were planning to develop skiing techniques that would allow them to beat Sandy down the mountain. The twins were studying the dictionary to have access to an infinite amount of words so they could beat the buddies at Scrabble more often.

Competition was not the most important thing in their lives. Their caring for each other was far more important for them than winning. In fact, they would help each other with Scrabble, slow down on the slopes for the "dragger," cook and wash dishes for their club of four and do it all with joy.

Perhaps the most amazing thing happening was that each member of the Friends Club was falling in love with another member, although they never revealed what the Love Angel had bestowed on them. They would never treat anyone better than another. Each said to themselves, *I guess I'm the only one that the Love Angel has poked, so I'd better just be quiet and enjoy this great party.*

But this was all going to change. An event would soon occur that would open each one's eyes and reveal the wonderful hidden thoughts going on in each friend's consciousness.

What's that guy doing up my tree?

Chapter XXX

It was a beautiful autumn Saturday night and before enjoying their traditional supper and Scrabble evening, they sat on the twins' porch to gaze in awe at the stars majestically strewn over the cloudless dark blue sky.

Laura joyfully expressed her feelings, "Isn't this incredible? I'm beginning to feel it is not just a coincidence that stars are all over our sky shining brilliantly to give us such pleasure."

"Yeah," Bryan responded, "God has given us such a great gift! I wonder how He does it? Maybe in Heaven we will find out."

Chad commented, "Oh, I want so much to believe in Heaven but, what proof do we have that Heaven exists?"

Sandy answered, "Chad, haven't you read Dr. Eben Alexander's *Proof of Heaven*? It sold millions of copies and no better qualified person could have written about the subject. After suffering from a disease he acquired in Israel, he was in a coma for seven days. The doctors had little hope he would ever wake, and if he did there was only a two percent chance, he could ever move again. He came back to life in perfect health and wrote this book about his journey. There are many 'after life' experiences that have been documented, but I think because he was a brain surgeon his story had more credibility than other writers."

"Really, maybe I'll get it," Chad pledged.

Then Bryan urged the family, "Let's start on our next assignment...supper." And they all headed into the house smiling.

"The lasagna is ready. Just perfect," Laura, the good cook, announced.

Chad got the salad out and after they all got settled at the table, Chad said grace. "Okay, Lord, if you really are out there, I want to tell you we are really grateful for this food and for bringing us together tonight—and all the nights we have enjoyed together."

They all smiled and dug in. The dinner was great and Laura said, "This is all so wonderful. Something special is going on here."

They ate all the delicious food and cleaned up the kitchen, and then rushed into the living room and got out the Scrabble board.

"What better way to end the evening?" Laura asked.

"The best way to end the evening is for me to win," Bryan joked.

They each picked their seven letters, and Sandy got an "A" again so she had to come up with the first word. They were quiet as they pondered what was going to be the best way to use their letters. They were all so focused on their next assignment that they didn't look over at the video screen on Laura's phone. They should have. There was a loud crash as the door was knocked open.

A young man walked in and held a pistol which he kept

pointing back and forth at them. As he began to speak, he directed the gun at Chad, "Chad, I am Tony, and you have ruined my life. Because of the success of your work, I lost my job. I have no money. I have nothing, and you are the reason why. The only solution I have now is to end your life...and mine."

The moment Tony entered the room with his gun, Bryan grabbed Laura and got in front of her. Chad did the same with Sandy, but Sandy slipped loose and stood up and slowly walked toward Tony with a beautiful smile on her face and looked up at him. Tony was more than six feet tall and Sandy was just a little over five feet.

With a smile Sandy said, "Tony, do you realize God loves you so much? God sees you as His beloved son as He sees us all. We all here in this room see you as a beloved child of God. And I know God is going to provide for your every need—as He has done with all of us here in this room."

Laura and Chad had expressions of awe on their faces. *How can Sandy be so loving to a man whose intent is to destroy us all?* were their thoughts.

Bryan just looked up and prayed knowing deeply that God was ever present.

Tony was silent. The expression on his face was one that seemed to convey a feeling of confusion.

"Tony, you are welcome to join us here this evening. We will all love you as God loves you," Sandy stated with great warmth and gently touched Tony's shoulder.

Tony dropped the pistol on the floor and slowly, looked up to "Heaven," and started walking out the front door.

"When you are feeling comfortable, come back and see us. You will always be welcome. God is speaking to me. God who loves us is telling me to bless you. So, I am. You have become the real, wonderful Tony, you have always been," Sandy lovingly said.

Then Tony disappeared. Sandy with prayerful hands, smiled and looked up and said, "Thank you dear Father for guiding me this evening." Then she sat on a couch and closed her eyes. Chad sat down next to her and put his arm around her, and then Bryan and Laura held hands and sat across from Chad and Sandy.

After a long period of silence, Chad spoke with tears in his eyes. "Coincidence is no longer my God. The God of Love is my God. Father, forgive my ignorance of what was always really true. Thank you for your love for all five of us."

After a few minutes of silence, Laura spoke, "Thank you Lord, for taking this challenging time to teach us the reality of life which is that you are Love. This evening your Love encompassed all of us. I have earnestly striven to have faith. Tonight, you have given it to me and Chad."

Quietly and slowly they all got up and put their arms around each other. Then Laura took Bryan's hand and said, "Let me walk you to your car.

Sandy, looked up at Chad, took his hand and said, "Okay, Chad, from now on I'm going to be your escort and always walk you to your car." Chad said, "Let's walk one another together." Everyone smiled because they had learned so much that evening. They also knew how much they cared for each other, and they learned who had become very special in their hearts.

Sandy said, "I'm reminded of Zephaniah 3:15: 'Even the Lord is in the midst of thee, thou shalt not see evil anymore.'"

Bryan softly added, "This quote that I recently read from

Ludwig von Beethoven's diary certainly seems relevant to all we have discussed for the last year, 'It was not a fortuitous meeting of chordal atoms that made the world. If order and beauty are reflected in the constitution of the universe, then there is a God.'"

Then even softer, Sandy quoted John, 4:8: "'For God is Love.' And from Numbers 14:21, 'All the earth shall be filled with the glory of the Lord.'" Then Sandy added, "And I just know there is something so wonderful, that will appear, beyond all that we are even perceiving at this moment. As it says in Acts 17: 28: 'For in him we live and move and have our being.' So in truth we must live in the consciousness of the Lord."

Soon the twins' neighbors, who had previously brought them flowers, joined the gang for Scrabble. Then Suzy Patrich, the woman who AAA helped in the snowstorm, accepted the Gang's invitation to have some fun playing Scrabble with them all.

And guess what?

Two weeks later, Tony showed up and asked if could join them.

Lovely Aspen trees on the mountain overlooking Steamboat.

Epilogue

Even though *Are You Kidding?* is a fictional novel, so much that happens in this book has actually happened to the author in real life while he was living in Steamboat Springs, Colorado.

I was almost attacked by a mother brown bear. She came out of some bushes about eight feet away while I was trying to take a picture of her cub who had just disappeared into the bushes. I raised my arms and growled, and the bear ran away. I only got scared later, but I was also incredibly grateful that God guided me with what to do with my arms.

Also, one night I drove through the center of a herd of elk at high speed because I couldn't slowdown in time, but my car didn't touch any animal as I passed through the herd. This was just as it happens to the friends in the book.

The author also became acquainted with the real mayor of Oak Creek, Cargo Rodeman, and was extremely impressed by all she was able to accomplish.

While biking in California Park, I did not notice a mountain lion until after I put my bike on the rack on my car and started to drive away. For several minutes a beautiful mountain lion raced along with me right next to the driver's side of the car. I think he was sorry that he had not jumped on me before I got safely in my car. So, I didn't have to experience the fright that Laura suffered when the mountain lion races beside her bike in the book.

I was also struck by a snowboarder, as Chad was, and was hurled ten feet down the mountain. By the grace of God, I, like Chad, suffered no injuries.

I've also gone over Devil's Causeway many times and have never fallen off. But, I did do something very stupid once. I thought it would be fun if I crossed the whole way without touching the rocks, but step from one rock to the next with my hands up in the air. My son, Michael, who was with me at the time, refused to look at me and turned away and faced in the opposite direction. I guess he didn't want to see his crazy dad fall down into the canyon. I made it safely across, thank the Lord. Maybe next time I'll try doing it blindfolded. *Are you kidding?*

But probably the most meaningful real-life scene in the book is at the end when Sandy lovingly talks with Tony who is threatening to kill Chad and his friends. Though this scene never happened to me personally, similar scenes have occurred to a multitude of people over the years. One example is a testimony similar to what Sandy experienced which David Degler relates in the *Christian Science Sentinel*, November 26, 2001, "You are Always Safe in God's Care." The testimony describes a woman who faced a man with a gun pointed at her.

> *This testimony is about a teenager who was forced to get into her car with a man who threatened her with a gun. He had just escaped from prison and ordered her to drive out of town.*
>
> *She prayed, to know that God loved them both. She continued to pray for them both while the man held*

her at gunpoint all night. When daylight came, the man stopped his threatening, let her drive back into town and left her unharmed.

This entire testimony, as well as many similar ones, can be read in the article listed previously by visiting any Christian Science Reading Room.

Elk River before the snow arrives.

If you agree with the message, I would be so grateful if you were to pass on this book or suggest others to order it from Amazon using my name as the author.

Any comments regarding *Are You Kidding?* can be sent to the author at jsant@zirkel.us.

With my deepest gratitude I wish to thank Bette Carlson, my-son-in-law Gary Albright, Jan and Joe McDaniel, Nancy Harris, Valerie Davia, Mark Robinson, Cargo Rodeman, and Gregory Block for all the help they provided me to produce this book.